Asombrosos anim...

HORMIGAS

T0014328

By Bray Jacobson
Traducido por Diana Osorio

Gareth Stevens
PUBLISHING

Please visit our website, www.garethstevens.com. For a free color catalog of all our high-quality books, call toll free 1-800-542-2595 or fax 1-877-542-2596.

Library of Congress Cataloging-in-Publication Data

Names: Jacobson, Bray, author.
Title: Hormigas / Bray Jacobson.
Description: New York : Gareth Stevens Publishing, [2022] | Series: Asombrosos
   Animalitos | Includes index.
Identifiers: LCCN 2020006184 | ISBN 9781538269015 (paperback) | ISBN
   9781538269022 (6 Pack) | ISBN 9781538269039 (library binding) | ISBN
   9781538269046 (ebook)
Subjects: LCSH: Ants–Juvenile literature.
Classification: LCC QL568.F7 J34 2022 | DDC 595.79/6–dc23
LC record available at https://lccn.loc.gov/2020006184

First Edition

Published in 2022 by
Gareth Stevens Publishing
111 East 14th Street, Suite 349
New York, NY 10003

Translator: Diana Osorio
Editor, Spanish: Rossana Zúñiga
Designer: Katelyn E. Reynolds

Photo credits: Cover, p. 1 Danita Delimont/ Gallo Images / Getty Images Plus; p. 5 Luis Diaz Devesa/
Moment/Getty Images; p. 7 arlindo71/E+/Getty Images; pp. 9, 24 (colony) Bryan Jones / EyeEm/Getty
Images; pp. 11, 24 (nest) Philippe Intraligi / EyeEm/Getty Images; p. 13 Giuseppe Zanoni/Moment/
Getty Images; p. 15 xu wu/Moment/Getty Images; p. 17 Stephane Pattiera / EyeEm/Getty Images; p. 19
ABimagestudio / iStock / Getty Images Plus; pp. 21, 24 (queen) Kaan Sezer/ iStock / Getty Images Plus;
p. 23 TheDman/ iStock / Getty Images Plus.

Printed in the United States of America

Some of the images in this book illustrate individuals who are models. The depictions do not imply actual
situations or events.

CPSIA compliance information: Batch #CS22GS: For further information contact Gareth Stevens, New York, New York at 1-800-542-2595.

Find us on

Contenido

Las hormigas son insectos pequeños.

Tienen tres partes
del cuerpo.

Viven en groupos.
Estas son colonias.

Las hormigas
construyen nidos.

Pueden estar hechos
de tierra.
Pueden estar hechos
de madera.

Las hormigas obreras
limpian el nido.
Ellos mantienen
la colonia segura.

Las hormigas obreras buscan comida.

Las hormigas comen
plantas y semillas.
¡Comen casi
de todo!

Las hormigas Reinas
ponen huevos.

21

Los bebes se toman
semanas en crecer.

23

Palabras que debes aprender

colonia

nido

Reina

Índice